THE ONE

BY

BOB MUSTIN

GRIDLEY FIRES

Copyright © 2018 Bob Mustin.

ISBN: 978-1-64204-292-4

All rights reserved. No part of this book may be produced or transmitted in any form, or by any means, electronic or mechanical, including photocopying, or by any information storage system, without permission in writing from the publisher or author.

First Published by *Gridley Fires Books*, 2/15/2018

GRIDLEY FIRES
THE BEST OF NEW SOUTHERN WRITING

Gridley Fires Books and its logo are
trademarked
by
Gridley Fires Books Publishing

Table of Contents

Divisions..............................1

Encounters
    History...........................8
    Herstory........................12

The Union........................16

DIVISIONS

Morning sun, warm my heart.
Where is the smile
that always thrills me so,
or must I resign myself
to the raucous music I hear
bouncing over the waves?
Please! Let your own lyric wash
over me like a new reality.

And what need have I
of a new reality? I think
there's need enough
in the early morning chill
to root me in this world forever.
I will not rise above the waves,
shivering, and beg a substitute
for what's already mine.

      Have you seen the clouded
      horizon? Cold rain slants
      over distant waters.
      Can you recall The One?

Mighty sea, mother of waters,
I did once rise above your waves,
and dark forces spirited me
away to a shining city, streets
covered with the salts
of imperious science.
It was there I lost myself
in idleness and poverty.

Do you abide such lassitude?
Only under the spell of
contemplative moments.
Infinite sea, your boundaries taste
the world at every latitude.
For the sake of my illumination,
why does my awe of you
seem so much like fear?

> One might fall walking
> barefoot through the sands
> of such a world. Would
> The One treat you so?

I've abandoned friends for this,
my surrender to your waves.
I baptize myself, then dive
to calmer depths where
something of the past endures.
A wave tosses me landward,
tumbling and rolling with salt
on my tongue and sand in my suit.

Is it really possible to be born
anew in each moment
in these self-same bodies,
wave after wave,
resisting the undertow,
water spewing from my nose?
I fear I'm a silly knave destined
to learn the same lessons over and over.

> What do you know of the sun,
> the solar orb of Helios?
> does his face remind
> you of The One?

I walk the crystal sands,
watch the crabs dance,
living their measure of life.
Here at water's edge,
the moveable frontier,
neither sea nor sand exist.
Here, new elemental forces
are bent on being born.

Dare I speak of what is real
in such a place?   Perhaps not.
Then hang reality, I ask for silence.
But a fertile mind knows
no silence. It's an ocean
of thought, torrents of it,
spreading its fantasies across
a world of time and space.

> The day quickens.
> Do you hear the echoing gulls?
> A cloud of hearts
> beating within The One.

Grand paradox, hydrous stone, Goddess
Earth, you are indeed fabulous.
I join the crabs in their
synchronous moment
and follow the surf
to a bandstand. The musicians
return from their smokes and drinks,
and I ask a young woman to dance.

We glide across the sand,
touching indiscreetly. I hardly know her
but a tension escalates between us.
I'm afraid it's all too obvious,
embarrassing, like the careless
talk of an old married couple.
Such a sunset I say, and she whispers.
Yes, I reply, I'll come up for tea.

> Shall we stop this silly ritual
> and get down to business?
> The night moves – will it take
> the two of us to The One?

Darkness has fallen, the sky's
a universe of wind and mystery.
Select a star, she says, one of red or blue
(They lurk in the moon's
penumbra, winking
from a faroff perch). Let's scramble
aboard and ride it. Now doesn't that seem
familiar, like a childhood carousel?

And just how long have you known
I yearn to race from star to star
leaping the voids between
succeeding moments –
Hands and feet – already gone!
This frail vessel dreams
of being a supernova
formless, fulfilled and free.

>It's a spiral path.
>Take a fleeting look
>through my kaleidoscope
>and glimpse The One.

We spend the night stoned,
beguiled. We're in the grasp
of rapture and it is deep.
We long for the clear view –
can the shoreline
be made straight? It's destiny
most divine that has drawn us
to this place, to one another,

but there are reasons why
we remain separate,
a polarized pair. Still, we have
this passion for one another.
Mountains and valleys tremble
as we tremble, and something
slow to dawn remains unspoken.
Tell me, what secrets do you hide?

> Beautiful morning,
> the sun has baked us quite
> a pudding to consider. Shall we
> breakfast on The One?

Encounters

History

Hummocks on this mountain rising –
my garden, goddess, bounty
from seeds exploding.
Harvest me like gravity
if some errant wind wishes
to carry me away,
and off we go, inventing
orbits about one another
somewhere in the cold, dark
freedom of the Appalachians.
Some call it adventure,
I call it Eden as we
settle with caution
into this virgin country,
the alliance of two
participating hearts,
full of hope, willing
to talk to one another,
never to be sure, perhaps,
of who we are, together.

Is that your voice echoing
among the poplar leaves,
hollow inside a child's
pennywhistle? I must confess
such sounds are not burned
into my memory.
What are they called?
Songs? Mutterings?
Whatever their nature
they must quiet
if I'm to know
the core of you. There,
truth runs strong and pure;
I must be sure these sounds
are yours alone, that the story
you expect me to write,
the story of my dreaming
of worlds complete
and eternal, is free
of all corruption.

No? We're resolved
to grapple with this scarp
in silence from separate handholds?
Will you at least take your rest with me?
The wind will leave us naked
of everything unreal,
but we will be warm
in one another, the wind
transformed into whispers,
your breath and mine,
our only fear
in never knowing
where you end and I begin.
So tell me, where is your garden?
Is this one yours or mine?
The perplexity of that so freeing,
like smoke from a spent candle,
and we must now shed
our human selves,
only pure spirit remaining.

We linger for a moment, waiting –
the bonds that separate us hold.
Why have I come for you?
Is it some earthly fixation,
or a divine appointment
we must keep,
keeping us alive,
leaving us complete, if only
for the moment of our service?
If I ask for more than this
I dare not take less –
what a mess, it seems,
to act out the play
and never know
the lines until I feel them
tumbling from my mouth.
There's something more to be
made of our encounter.
Can we press the pieces
of this puzzle together?

HERSTORY

Loving you takes willfulness,
but it's as certain as the seasons.
Does time matter, then?
Your love for me flashes
like summer lightning.
I feel it shake me;
I see its intermittent light
engraved on the starry path
that led you to this mountain.
But the pathway to me
is steep and treacherous,
not to be traversed
in a moment. So come,
leave your bombast
in my garden;
exhausted, sleep
beside me the slumber
of unknowing. Steadfastness
lies satisfied only in the final
gasp of passion.

Don't you know I've been here
always, waiting with patience
among the mountain spires
and the eagle nests?
I'm the morning fog,
the mystery that imagines
you an exotic species. I'm here
and always will be, but then
I'm everywhere,
everywhere you go.
No moments lie
untouched, no thought
unturned, no movement made
is without my cause. I have known
you beyond this veil
of space and time,
never seeing you –
more like a memory,
the gentleness of your soul
somehow finding, touching mine.

So are you a figment,
a dream? No, you're real,
calling softly, almost
lost within the magic
of a single moment.
We must come together
in this place called time,
in which nothing may stand
save change itself.
We must return
to our beginnings – can we
redirect the tides of time?
It's not for us to point
the direction the path
human imperfection takes;
only to walk it, step
by step, allowing
the ever-changing winds
to urge us on, to make
of each stride a new truth.

Your concerns are not mine.
My certainty reaches
deep into the well
of possibility, your
lightning far into
the chasm of sleepless
dreaming, your thunder
loosening the dream we both
have dreamed, clothing it
in humble apparel.
Wake up!
I'm with you at last.
It's only been the fear
of never meeting,
the strangeness of having
no illusions, that kept
my hand from yours.
Shedding our misgivings,
we walk, leaves of light
falling in our wake.

THE UNION

The distance between us
will close, slowly,
like breezes drifting
across a star-laden sky –

transparent stagehands sweeping
away clouds, revealing
soft patches of light filling
the circle of a rising moon.

The life we live is similar light,
quiet fingers passing
through prisms of form,
creating a rainbow of the senses,

urging us on, always reaching,
never quite able to touch
the truth of what we really are.
They circumscribe us,

these nimble fingers – they dance,
weave tapestries of song,
tell wondrous stories, amaze
us with science and magic,

then fall to our sides,
tired from their exertions
in the viscous night
of constant change,

reborn as the clear light,
the most immutable light
carrying our seed, the faint
chemistry we are.

So let us understand
this moment, savor its presence,
remember, we are something
splendid to one another,

watch the lunar light
reach out and touch
wet crystals hanging
from each uncounted leaf,

watch the alchemical
transformation as they drop
like the shining filaments
the spider leaves,

wetting our feet,
cooling our fears,
allowing us once more
to wade, to swim, to flow

with the rhythms,
the almost imperceptible
pulsations of life the earth
presents to us.

Do you see it all before you,
here, in each moment
we pass through?
I have seen us reach out

to seize such a moment,
hold it to our hearts
and never know the way
one instant becomes the next,

never know our yearnings
for the past, the future,
keep us chained here
to wait   to wait…

There! On the stage
some magic has set before us –
this distant lunar beauty,
this cool, clear reflection

of our one composite life,
drifts quietly past,
as would a boat on a river,
a boat carrying gods,

and it passes like spun gold
through the forested poplars,
the naked sentinels
that mark our passing,

the journey set in motion
so long ago. And one by one
we choose. Look!
The movement among

the slenderest trees?
There's much embracing
And some leave swimming
(so swiftly it seems like flying)

toward the lunar boat.
The gods rejoice, welcome us
on board and we turn to wave
to those who choose to stay,

to wait among the trees
for fortune's graces
to smile on another day.
But choices are made, in truth,

only with open eyes,
with a conscious awareness
that all is well   that all is well,
and in this moment

we encounter the river   the void,
the broad expanse before us.
We feel its currents,
we hear its muted whisper,

and we choose our path
toward the horizon
moving in the manner of all life
toward The One.

But, we ask ourselves,
what has seeing this given us?
Are we the better for it?
We swoon deeply into contemplation,

for the question is a worthy one,
though there is no answer, really.
We only see, within this reverie,
that wherever the river goes

we go together –
wherever there is danger
we go, side by side,
allowing life to unfold,

to be discovered, assembled
from all perspectives,
into the many human
faces of The One.

We hear somewhere within
this moment the yet unspoken
voice of our becoming,
the sound of the egg breaking,

we see the labyrinth,
the lifestream we are,
pouring out its creations.
We feel the tremble of birth

and we know, through this
our last communion, the full range
of our experience,
the complete and total being

from which we come.
We see the sense
in the wild expanse
of our diversity,

and in this moment of revelation,
which is constant, eternal, we see
that many paths are joined here.
With eyes open wide,

we pour our very lives
into the ecstasy, the new freedom
realized in knowing
we are once again The One.

ABOUT THE AUTHOR

Bob Mustin has had a brief naval career and a longer one as a civil engineer and has been a North Carolina Writers Network writer-in-residence at Peace College under the late Doris Betts' guiding hand. In the early 90s he was the editor of a small literary journal, The Rural Sophisticate, based in Georgia. His work has appeared extensively in print and electronic publications.

To learn more about Bob Mustin, visit:
Website: www.bobmustin.com
Blog: bobmust.wordpress.com

www.ingramcontent.com/pod-product-compliance
Lightning Source LLC
Chambersburg PA
CBHW030237100526
44584CB00015BB/1601